Lost in the Telling

Harold Whit Williams

FUTURECYCLE PRESS
www.futurecycle.org

Library of Congress Control Number: 2015935871

Copyright © 2015 Harold Whit Williams
All Rights Reserved

Published by FutureCycle Press
Lexington, Kentucky, USA

ISBN 978-1-938853-66-1

For Scott Alexander Jones

I'm just speaking out loud to cancel my silence.
Consider it an old impulse, doomed
to become mere words.

—*Stephen Dunn*

Contents

I

A Time of Drought..9
A Rum-Drunk Toast After Raking Oranges
    from a Neighbor's Tree, and Ending with
    a Banal Line from a Seventies Pop Song.....................11
Requiem for Yourself or Someone Like You.....................12
It's What We're All Thinking...13
Light at the End of the Tunnel..14
A True North Dream with Astronomy
    and Botanical Consequences.......................................15
A Metaphysical Dream with Staff Meeting
    and Thunderstorm..16
A Recurring Death Dream with Songbird
    and Prescription Medication..17
A Lover's Dream with Crop Duster, Football Game,
    and a Dancing Shetland..18
Gunwaleford Road Pastoral..19
Blues Dreams..20
Script Notes for a Blues Dream..22
Last Blue Yodel..23
All Jam Bands to the Moon..24
In a Sentimental Mood..25
Watchmaker God's Eureka Moment....................................26
Watchmaker God's Luminosity Curve................................27
Watchmaker God, Asleep on the Clock,
    Dreams It All Up from Beginning to End..................28
Still Life with Student Cello and Turntable......................29
Still Life with Gibson SG and Unpacked Bags.................30
Still Life with Marvel Archtop and Shure SM57..............31
A Correspondence of Sorts...32
Lost in the Telling...33

II

Root of the Problem...37
Neon Yellow Pillow Fight..39
What Brother Says..40
Winston County Bottom Feeders...41
Five Extra Minutes...42
Our Lord and Savior's Mixtape..44
The Dream/Life of Relics..45
Ballad of a Late Bloomer...46
Ciudad Mante Firebreather..47
Stompbox Coordinates..48
Wasted on the Young...50
Daywork Near a Bend in the Tennessee River....................51
Recently Discovered Field Notes of the Texas Naturalist..................52
Despite or Because of the Bourbon......................................55
Tottenham Street Blues..56
Villanelle for Extinct Birds...57
English Sonnet for Extinct Birds...58
Ghazal for Extinct Birds..59
Bedtime Story Redux..60
Bar Napkin Love Letter...61
Time Out...62
Day After Christmas Blues Poem..63
The Only Apocalypse..64
Notes on the Year's End..65
Acknowledgments

I

A Time of Drought

Sometimes I hear it raining
When it's not raining sometimes
Sleep evades me like thunder-
Heads skipping over fields
Of knee-high corn stalks
Little brown fingers pointing
Accusing sky of negligence
And when I do drift off I
Dream that I pray for rain
And it rains on me sleeping
My roots go deep and I wake
From dreamsleep fully clothed
I will leaf out and blossom

A Rum-Drunk Toast After Raking Oranges from a Neighbor's Tree, and Ending with a Banal Line from a Seventies Pop Song

To Ron Zacapa and Che Guevara, to Carmen
Miranda and our Miranda rights, to Rites
Of Spring and the Arab Spring and what we
Sing in the shower, to the meaning of your

Name and all that mine rhymes with, to
The gods of Popol Vuh, to old Chano next
Door and Banana Man on the corner, to
Your flashing Mayan temper and my inbred

British chin, to the ache in our shoulders
And the splinters we'll dig out tomorrow,
To the soft laughter of backporch women,
To the cotton candy sunset and the *beer beer*

Call of nighthawks, to the thudding of each rain-
Plumped fruit into the freshly cut St. Augustine.
O friend, *mi diablo*! Our glasses are emptied—
Nothing lasts forever but the earth and sky.

Requiem for Yourself or Someone Like You

It will be easy enough to pass away
When the time comes. Nary a word
About nothingness. What's hard
Is living the day-to-day drama

Right down to the molecular level—
Offhand remarks digging like thorns
Into the side. That gray sky blue sky

Don't ask me why godless expanse
Above our heads. The same words,
The same words. What if I've been
Dead wrong about everything?

When do I wake up to this dream?
Verily I say unto thee, the soul that
Cannot dance will surely not move on.

It's What We're All Thinking

after Alvin Aubert

Did you spy that housefly in the casket?
It flew in right before the lid was closed.
O the pancake make-up, the sewn-up lips!
And just what was her final meal? I'll bet
Fishsticks or microwave mac and cheese.

And just what were her final words? I heard—
Roll it to the street, damn it, it's Wednesday.
She kept the television on all night long.
She kept his only suit pressed and laid out.

She drove herself to church, bat-blind
And full of road-rage. She always said—
If you let them, they'll screw you good.
She always said—if you listen to rain
Late at night, it will leave you lonelier.

Light at the End of the Tunnel

We're nearing the part of the high school play
Where the leading man finds a letter—his lover
Long gone, bound for shimmering city lights.
We're fast approaching the final track of Side 2—

A brooding, introspective fingerpicked folk
Melody flowing into furious amp feedback.
We've dropped below a quarter of a tank, love,
And this pineywoods highway has nothing

But churches. We've awakened on our porch
And the lawn is lush from last night's rain.
In the blooming redbud tree, a sparrow sings—
I can see for miles and miles and miles and miles...

A True North Dream with Astronomy and Botanical Consequences

Somewhere along the trail, this
Flashlight becomes a femur, and I
Take that for a sign. Like when moss
Grows on the north side of trees
Except when it grows on all sides.
Or when the Big Dipper cannot
Be spotted through those freakish
Superstorm clouds. Should I mention
Sleepwalking runs in my family?
All I can say is that each day
Is a cool copse of virgin spruce
Where I forage and grow musky.
And before long, my fingers leaf out.
I become rooted beside a brook
That refuses to babble my name.
Eventually, it speaks when I bare
My spindly branches for winter.
It murmurs—All I've ever wanted
Was to find my way back home.

A Metaphysical Dream with Staff Meeting and Thunderstorm

It happens during a fire drill,
A campus poetry reading,
A run-of-the-mill afternoon
When a coworker says *attrition*
And *team player* and *word cloud*.
I picture this free verse floating
Above my mind's rolling pasture.
Lie back in the dry sage grass
Of a summer ages ago and spy
This thing shape-shift, expand,
Overtake and swallow midday sun.
Sky darkens, air cools, a south wind
Kicks up quail. The first fat drops
Dissolve in red dust, but soon
I'm soaked through to some metaphor
For bones. Washed clean of words.
Born again beneath the bottom line.

A Recurring Death Dream with Songbird and Prescription Medication

There is always the old woman
And the older woman waiting.
Morning rain shower steaming
Off the sun-bright highway. A jay
Squawking high in the maple
By the steaming highway. Always
The old woman setting out lunch,
The older woman swallowing
Meds with cold coffee. Maple
And the jay, sun-bright highway
Steaming. There is always prayer
And the whisperings of prayer.
Hydrangeas showy by the porch.
A seeking in the Scriptures,
Index finger licked and stabbed
Repeatedly, flicking thin pages.
A darkening sky with thunder
To the west. There is always
The old woman washing up,
The older woman not breathing,
Turning the deep blue of hydrangeas,
Of jays, of an ever-shrinking sky.

A Lover's Dream with Crop Duster, Football Game, and a Dancing Shetland

If I could scrape up enough dosh
For that skywriter's cost
Our names would hover high
Inside a chem-trail heart—
HAROLD LOVES ASHLEY
Dissipating from a westerly
Into BAROLO DONBA ABBOZ
Above a homecoming game
Half-time extravaganza.
Either that or splurge and rent
A magical seaside pony
To stamp in surf and sand
And tell our fortunes in dance.
We clap hands and sing along
With seagulls and wind gusts
And promise to carry out
Those things he had predicted.
We return him many years later
And do not get charged a fee.

Gunwaleford Road Pastoral

It can all turn south in the blink of an eye,
In a flutter of bird wings, in the butterfly
Oak leaf wind gust. Once, I pulled a red wagon
That rattled with fossils; now I groan and wheeze
When the alarm sounds. Each day is either

A cloud wisp skirting the cathedral spire
Or another sandstone stacked on the burial cairn.
In geologic time, both blip past unnoticed.
They say rainfall patterns fluctuate according to

Yahweh's whimsy. This gives us plenty to discuss
At the general store. Around a woodstove
We gather with RC Colas and moon pies,
All asking the same question while using
Different tones and accents and words.

Blues Dreams

for Hubert Sumlin

Born Under a Bad Sign

Along the way somebody hefted an axe
And took some whacks against my family tree.
Those dead-branch second cousins, those
Low-hanging aunts and uncles gone
Soggy and rotten—they all had it coming.
To this day I bay like the neighbor's cur
Drunken from the fermented windfalls.
I droop and dream of Daddy's orchard,
All the shiny and soft pears and plums.
Honeybees up in the sun-bright blossoms.
Each trunk weatherworn, bug-scarred.
Each fruit wearing a face I'll fondly forget.

Mannish Boy

And another time Daddy says look
Out the window, not my window,
Your window, the one that's cracked,
The one that's half-open and hazy
From mud splatter and field grit.
The one letting in those raindrops,
Fat and salty, falling from gulf clouds.
See that crooked old house yonder
Leaning behind the Texaco pump?
They say the ghost of Lovely Lloyd
Haints the front-porch rocking chair,
Hollering and waving at fast-passing
Traffic bound for Tupelo or Jasper
Or Bear Creek or Nauvoo. Wave back
At Lloyd, son, he baited your hooks.
He let you ring up the cash register.
His wife Martha wiped your ass once.

Another Mule Kicking In My Stall

At this juncture the river is too wide,
Too swift and too strong. A bottleneck
Slide scraped along taut catgut strings
That sing and moan like a crop-beaten
Beast of burden. Cry *gee,* then cry *haw.*
Cry over evil deeds done at midnight.
What a sight! This Old Muddy flooding
Fields, lapping the levee. I'll get there
Somehow, someway, and on that day
You'll be sorry you've done me wrong.
My High John the Conqueror root,
My gris-gris bag, my thirty-eight special
Hot in my hand. I just quit that band,
Burnt down your house of blues. You
Say two of us forever, but my aim is true.

See That My Grave Is Kept Clean

Salt these wounds, my sweaty friend,
And let the noise begin with Elmore,
Blind Lemon, Muddy and all the Kings.
Men do feel the need to be useful
Even when low on gas, passed out,
Flaccid, drunk upon scuffed hardwoods.
I'll be good by tomorrow morn.
Your sneer, your scorn is my rye
Whiskey and draft beer. Do you hear
Sonny Boy's harp out of tune and yet
Perfect? Do you taste champagne, smell
The reefer? Can't you see? Sooner or
later we all live our blues. We enter
That cutting contest bound to lose.

Script Notes for a Blues Dream

The camera pans down the levee.
Big river roiling, coffee-colored
And angry. Pans to a shack at the edge
Of a flooded field. Zooms in slow
To a man on the porch. Dungareed.
Way down south he hangs his hat.
Beneath the Mason and the Dixon.
Where the Southern cross the Dog.
He's a rice farmer or a cotton farmer,
A barge hand or a vagabond. In his
Reoccurring night visions, a bird
Comes to visit his bedside. Let's say
A mockingbird, but gigantic. This rube,
This field hand, he shot his old woman.
Flashback to the scene. Motel room
With blood and brains on the wall.
He says—*She got what comin' to her.*
He says—*I do it again if I havin' to.*
Dream mockingbird stands six feet tall.
Sings—*I'm gonna buy me a pistol
With a great long shiny barrel. Gonna shoot
That rounder who stole away my gal.*
Dreambird sings—*Baby please don't go
Down to New Orleans...*camera fades into
Morning, sunshine on the hollyhocks.
Town sheriff knocks down the back door,
Hauls this outlaw off to jail. Judge, jury,
Executioner. This deadbeat, this hoodlum
Steps up to the noose, says—*Whatever
Weight you choose in this world, make
Sure it pulls you all the way down.*

Last Blue Yodel

Let us both huddle around
That little golden fire
Inside the whiskey bottle.

Each sip, a breath of smoke.
Let us bow, pray to weather—
That hard norther howling,

Pawing at our windows.
Let us yawn and stretch
And down the last dram.

Let the remainder of my life
Be a library paperback, one
You toss in the backseat

And never return. Let us
Nod off and snore as my
Beard goes a winter-sky gray.

Let Jimmie Rodgers skip
On our thrift store turntable—
Woman made a fool out of me...

Woman made a fool out of me...
Woman made a fool out of me...

All Jam Bands to the Moon

"In Memory of Elizabeth Reed" had my favorite solo
Until I heard the painted bunting sing.
Bunting me this, bird enthusiast—is the mocking-
Bird born with riffs, or are they acquired over time?
Most likely, it's not either/or, as I on occasion
Holler out like calling hogs to slop, hollering
In the voice of my great granddaddy a century ago,
A dirt farmer busting up stumps in his field,
Some kind of palsied music belching from his mouth
On a Sunday morning. Yet other times my fingers
Flow over the fretboard in the well-worn grooves
Of the pentatonic blues, fuzz pedal dialed in
To a mongrel's snarl. But it's all been done,
And will continue to be overdone, and maybe
We're all done for when that spotlight shines
Down on the drum riser. Something tribal
And ancient and embarrassing about the extended
Drum solo—the singer backstage primping,
The lead guitarist having his ego stroked. In the time
It took you to read this, somewhere a band
Has reached maximum overdrive. Somewhere
A stage manager grimaces, glancing at his watch.

In a Sentimental Mood

Alive as ice melts in the backyard,
Neighborhood children caterwaul
A snow day. Ever a thinking man,

Considering all sides, comers, takers—
Could just as easily be dead with ice
Popping inside a whiskey tumbler.

Bluish hands licked by the house cat.
Two crows fussing a hawk up
And out of the oak. A low hum

From speakers finished blasting
Coltrane with Ellington. No one
Around to flip over Side One.

Watchmaker God's Eureka Moment

If only there was such a thing
As a songbird singing outside

The picture window, out inside
The pitch darkness of it all.

And that's it! A sunlit place
For a thing called a songbird

That sings from a budding
Branch or a building ledge. Lungs

Filling with air, tongue tweaking
The pitches that rise and fall

In through the picture window,
Into the place where darkness was.

Watchmaker God's Luminosity Curve

And then I said, let there be—what?
Sparklers hissing in childhood hands.

A backwoods campfire illuminating
High school kisses. Riverside luminarias.

Candles in the ice storm. They're all
Still glittering somewhere tonight. Tiny

Bullets hurtling through the cosmos.
And downtown and on the seashore

And in dewy fields at dusk, fireflies
Or heat lightning or a sheriff's spot-

Light flickers, then goes out. A Bic
Sparks up in the alley. The backlit

Red oak at sunrise. A light, the old
Song says, that shines from your eyes.

Watchmaker God, Asleep on the Clock, Dreams It All Up from Beginning to End

I am the Alpha and Omega, nodding off.
Sweet slumbers for this omnipotent nothing.

Bang—it was that big! Like a company truck
Backfiring on some Arkansas two-lane,

Wet snow deadening the stubblefields
To make it all seem much quieter. Bang—

Like a shotgun times twenty-five trillion
And then some. Roll over. Get comfy

Everybody, the night is young. And then
The stretching, the pulling of galactic taffy.

Star stuff cooling. Cells splitting, mutating.
Life begins to happen in the oddest places.

I snug the covers up over my godbeard
As rocks dance and shift in seismic fits. Light

Becomes brighter, heat hotter. Contraction.
An alarm goes off. Just hit snooze, sweet Lord.

Still Life with Student Cello and Turntable

I tune her low to make it sound like Mingus
Recording *Ah Um*. My index finger smarts
From plucking along to "Fables of Faubus,"
But that howling middle tenor sax imparts
A righteous pain I've never known and never
Will know. I thank the gods of jazz for that.
This music tumbles, dazzles. It's too clever
For the likes of me. On "Goodbye Porkpie Hat"
I spill my glass of wine. It stains the rug
Like virgin's blood—a sacrificial offering.
So maybe this is a sign. I pray and beg
To play it cool and hot, enlightened, wailing
The blues as if I could. I stroke and cajole
Those strings and try to get it in my soul.

Still Life with Gibson SG and Unpacked Bags

My fellow traveler, we should be committed!
Those days without sleep, the studio slog,
That Sisyphean loading out of abused
Equipment; luggage stolen; in the bag
To board a mid-morning London flight.
But what brave heroics, you and I—a Soho
Debut, our Radio One almost-hit,
A Marshall stack up loud to steal the show.
My blood and sweat are soaked into the wood
Around your pickup heart, your wiry veins.
A coat of paint that once was white is yellowed
From cigarette and reefer smoke and stains
Of god knows what. Let's toast the gypsy life,
The near and far misses, the trouble and strife.

Still Life with Marvel Archtop and Shure SM57

I'm thinking it's from the forties. Seems
A fitting decade for that hillbilly sound.
Those Carter Family and Jimmie Rodgers
Records have permeated the good land.
Hard, lean times mostly over; folks
Wanting a bit of music for themselves.
It might've gigged around—those cracks
Would indicate—or sat under shelves
At a Main Street general store, packed
Snug in its case away from dust and grime.
I pluck it gently on weekends, all miked
Up to capture a little moment in time,
A combination of chords that sways
A soul, that brightens the dark of days.

A Correspondence of Sorts

After midnight, a Ouija board and I
Write you a love letter. No invisible
Ink, though, so I make quick jotting
Gestures above the brittle parchment.

No empty bottle, no ocean to drop it in, so
I stay put, as this weather's turned atrocious.
The world outside my window? It could be
Endless in the dark. I should pretend
I'm you reading this letter out loud,

But I've no matches for the candle
And no candle for the candlelight,
And whatever it was I meant to say
Can be better said by not saying it.

Lost in the Telling

When our flat-screen TV
Becomes a slash pine campfire
I will whittle you a raven
That fits in your palm.

I will spin you tight yarns
About a time before sunset
Before this world became
A dark alley with broken glass.

Some things will get lost
In the telling, other things
Will be found out too late.
The woodsmoke will sing

And your little bird will fly
And night will burn off
Like some summer fog
The dry creek dreamt up.

II

Root of the Problem

Somewhere between waking
And forgetting lies our dream
Of heaven our fairy tale of
An everlasting streets paved
With gold try as I might
I cannot keep morning sun
In its place the dragonfly
On a pond the dove on the wire
Try as I might I cannot preserve
The musique concrète *of sparrow-*
Song creek water what else
Is there to say? There is only
So much sunset sky to see
And it is never enough

Neon Yellow Pillow Fight

Leaving Narita Airport, 1996

Konnichiwa, dear driver, please pull over.
I can't hold it any longer. Too much Asahi.
I would love to read and comprehend

Your road signs. This one might say—
The Sky Here Is A Facsimile Of Itself
That No One Bothers To Looks At.

That one over there might say—*Please*
Maybe Rock And Roll Goodbye Now.
I'm guessing your sky today is gunmetal gray

Because this cold weather feels like some
Slow cinema bullet. I would love to stand here
Waxing poetic about starling flocks overhead,

How they shapeshift their murmurations into
The likeness of Mount Fuji, or a stubby penis,
Or Emperor Hirohito's eyeglasses. I would love

To keep standing here, relieving my bladder
On your entire country, nourishing the fields
For that coming rice crop. I would love

To read a road sign that said—*Everything*
Will Be A-OK. I would love to, just once,
Someday see someone else's original sky.

What Brother Says

A murder of crows explodes
From a bloated deer carcass
On Highway 72, and I swerve
Through north Mississippi hill
Country counting the crosses
Of car-crash ghosts, thinking
What I need is to move closer
To home and what I need is for
Those untelevised autumn clouds
To dissipate into some common
Sunshine and what I really need is
An hour alone with that twenty-
Year-old Tuscaloosa cheerleader,
She in her uniform and myself
In a Tarzan loincloth with a fifth
Of Early Times, and what I really
Really need is for God to exist
And come into my life, but it's too late
For all that and I just missed our exit.

Winston County Bottom Feeders

The overstocked catfish pond sleeps
By Highway 43, south of Boar Tush.
In late morning heat, Daddy's daddy
Sits frail in his lawn chair. His leathery
Hands quiver a cane pole; his cracked
Talon-fingers reek of stink bait.
He whispers curses and incantations,
Beckoning the sly, whiskered creatures.
Whistling, jittery, Daddy spies swallows
Overhead, gorging on mosquitoes
Full of our just-sucked blood. Our
Go-juice, he calls it. From us to bug
To swallow to hawk to vulture to clay
To hay to Holstein, then back to us,
And where does all this end? Daddy's daddy
Drops his head to snore. Daddy hollers—
This is the day that the Lord hath made!
I scratch an elbow, itch and think—surely
This goodness and mercy shall fail me
All the days of my life, as I will dwell
In murky depths till the lure floats down,
The hook sinks in, the line draws taut...

Five Extra Minutes

after Wallace Stevens

Just before we lose power
That Slovenian point guard
Drains a three, shocking

The hometown crowd.
Our television goes dark.
Everything goes dark. But

It's overtime, momentum
Shifting to the away team,
All bearded, road-warriored.

On the couch, we wave at
Ourselves waving at ourselves
On the blackened TV screen.

Usually it's a transformer
Nearby—gusty winds—or
Sometimes a gray squirrel

Gnawing in too deep or a
Dead limb giving way. Home-
Town crowds have always

Frightened me a bit. One
Imagines Mussolini mid-court,
Egging everyone on, aiming

A T-shirt gun at upper-level
Seats, preening, farting into
The microphone. We all clap

Like seals at Sea World. We
Flop fat ass cheeks down
On cushions hand-stitched

By tiny brown people. We
Simply stare into screens to
Behold the nothing not there
And the nothing that is.

Our Lord and Savior's Mixtape

Highway 72 slithers and slinks
Like some serpent in the garden.
A Mercury Zephyr with half a tank.
Factory tape deck blasting R.E.M,
AC/DC and The Cult. Guns &
Roses. Little traffic from here
To Tishomingo. Surprise snow
Left around the catfish ponds.
Doublewides with Xmas lights.
A church, a Texaco, another church,
A shooting range. County line
Liquor stores, another church.
Fugazi and The Meat Puppets.
What exactly would Jesus do?
Don camouflage and carry an AK?
Backhand his Mary Magdalene
After a long and pointless day
At the chicken plant? Would he
Be offended by this Zeppelin
Track or just muss up his hair
In the rearview, laughing off
The irony? Would he lust after
That slutty red-haired cheerleader?
Would he say to her, *It's no secret
Who I am, just ask around*? Would
He kill the headlights on that flat
Stretch east of Iuka? Count to ten
Before switching them back on?
Might he say, *Brother, take this,
Thy wheel* or *Do unto others
Before they damn well do it to you*?

The Dream/Life of Relics

Do you ever wonder what happened
To those arrowheads? Tossed in a
Move? Lost in that flood? Tow-
Headed daddy was a tiny cracker boy
Who dug them up beside Bear Creek,

Sharp little flint pieces glinting
In moonlight between rows of knee-
High cotton. Clovis points, pottery
Shards. Crows cawing, whippoorwills.
The supper bell rings. A shoebox

Sits full on the back porch. Daddy's
Tucked in, dreaming of Geronimo.
Those sharp little flint pieces in moon-
Light—still humming from flight,
Contact with white-tailed buck meat.

Ballad of a Late Bloomer

My very first kiss, a dry-lipped disaster,
Was eagerly placed somewhere near
Or about the face of the town druggist's
Daughter who, flabbergasted and furious,
Promptly slammed her front porch door,

Shotgunning sound down the sleeping
Street of lawyers' and bankers' houses.
And next day, in the halls after class,
There was much snickering amongst

Those who had been frolicking and
Fondling and fingering for months,
If not years. So I ate my sandwich alone,
Outside, underneath the autumn boughs
Of maples leaves too red to look at.

Ciudad Mante Firebreather

after Miller Williams

Southward from the Rio Grande
We seek tropical birds.
Blue-gray tanagers in mango trees.
Red-crowned parrots on telephone poles.

Half a bottle of tequila
Into a dusty town zocalo,
The skinny brown boy appears.
On a darkened street corner

He's either fifteen or fifty.
Armed with lit torch, fuel-filled milk jug,
He swigs and kisses the flame,
Anoints passing cars with dragonbreath.

As we hand him wads of ones
He wipes a filthy rag across flammable lips,
Inquires in perfect English,
Is either of you a doctor?

Stompbox Coordinates

Old WLAY Radio Building, Valdosta, Alabama
Lat/Long 34N 87W

Like Roman ruins, post apocalyptic,
These cinderblocks remain. Ubiquitous
The kudzu, stereotypically in each crack
And crevice. Tom and I have filled our bellies
With muscadines from Daddy's vines. We clamber
Across what's left of a roof to view the mountain
Due south of us. It'll soon fade into umber
And orange in hue. We speak of Hugh, a friend
Who just this summer got his first guitar.
I've yet to play but feel the vibes beneath
My feet, beneath the shingles, melted tar.
The country, blues and gospel thump, this truth
Sent out upon airwaves. I'll learn and burn
These licks to light my hometown map in scorn.

Liberty Lunch, Downtown, Austin, Texas
Lat/Long 30N 97W

The alley beckons. A joint is passed but I
Decline—my hacking pollen cough is bad
Enough to warrant stares. This April day
Is dying in the west, a strip of red
Beyond the hills outside of town. The club,
It cues our presence to the stage, all guts
A-tremble, shaky hands. Our suits are fab
But I feel a fib. A day-job friend, he cuts
In line to stand before my feet and grins
And flashes devil hands when I let off
A heavy fuzzed-out riff. The song begins;
The singer wins the crowd and looks to laugh
When I sustain an overdriven slide.
My friend no longer grins, eyes open wide.

Ancienne Belgique, Opening Slot, Brussels, Belgium

Lat/Long 50N 4E

The tiny streets are fogged with briny scents
Of *moules-frites, fromage*. We gather 'round
The beer and bread. Those brothers from Oasis
Have called our bluff for sure—they dig our sound
Of Beatles, Stones and Who. The tape we sped
Or slowed has now been spun on XFM
And BBC. I covet this urbane, moped
Ennui of kids in line for Noel, Liam
And Wonderwall. The waiter brings more ale
To quench our Texas thirst. Then J lights up
A cig and speaks of touring, record sales
While picking on his chinnywig. This hoop
We'll tumble through, I think, is not on fire
But rarely seen. How did we get this far?

Big Bend National Park Open Mic

Lat/Long 29N 103W

Because there's not another car for miles
Around out here, it seems we're in a dream.
You laugh and punch the rental's radio dial
To "scan" and watch it spin for nothing. A calm,
Relaxing holiday break is what I need—
Guitar and amp packed up for this has-been.
Our tent is pitched. We grab binocs, food
For the trail, hike to spy Boquillas del Carmen
Siesta-ing at noon. The dirty streets are bare
Except for mongrels. Rio Bravo, they say,
Divides the deserts, mountains, cultures here.
This ghost town in the glasses view I'll try
To keep inside my heart the whole year long.
At camp, someone has slain an Eagles song.

Wasted on the Young

Here's to those smoke signals
Rising from recess cigarettes.
Here's to the heft and struggle
Of backseat bodies sweat-slickened,

Midnight car windows fogged.
A possum on the porch, an owl.
Ow, you say, *take it easy there.*

But these fingers will one day sing
Verily before kings and queens
And princes of popular music.
Music we hear in the elevator,

The pharmacy, the grocery store.
We sway before the seafood case,
A man wrapping our catfish filets.

As a boy, I caught a four-pounder
With cane pole and stink bait.
Grandmother sliced its shiny belly,
Yanked out guts onto newspaper.

They glistened in sunlight. Daubers
And yellow jackets on the icebox pie.
Her picnic table gave me splinters.

Daywork Near a Bend in the Tennessee River

after Charles Wright

Mouths to feed, dear Lord, mouths to feed.
We cannot eat those bald cypress knees,
Pockmarking and puzzling the shallows, nor
Drink from this current, swift with summer rains.

It shoots the poison arrows of water moccasins,
Carries our detritus to the sea, washes clean
The murky creek beds of our conscience.
All that's left is just shamefaced labor

In bright rows of cotton, soybeans and rice.
The swatting and sweating for filthy lucre.
And here, cresting the cliff, a bald eagle
Dive-bombs the white-capping surface.

He pulls in a rivercat, child-sized, struggling.
Snatch me up in your tree-tall talons, Lord!
Lift me high above the browbeating sun.
Pick clean my weary bones in some glory land!

Recently Discovered Field Notes of the Texas Naturalist

I. Concerning the Identification of Various Cloud Formations

Tuesday, May 4—My ninety-nine-year-old grandmother's voice
Keeps crackling to me through this little plastic device.

Magic in my hand. Her accent is the sound of a skillet
Sizzling bacon fat, a screen door slamming, hailstones

On a tin roof, backwoods church hollers. I catch words
Like *republican* and *tornado* and *kardashian* and *warning*.

That storm's path is just miles from her house. It grabs
And tosses truck-sized boulders like some Tolkien troll.

It lifts believer and nonbeliever alike up inside the swirl,
Rapturing them into a million tiny pieces. *Sweet Jesus*

But I had to hang up. There's this desperate garage band
Dry-humping away across the street. *Thump-thump*

My coffee's gone cold. *Thump-thump* no new emails.
Gray sky and a wind gust and *thump-thump* I want

To take an axe to their power supply like Pete Seeger
At Dylan's screeching Newport electric debut. I want

A year-long moratorium on all music—old, new, whatever.
Unhook the speakers, I say! Power down the amplifiers!

I want only the calls of doves and jays, that verse/chorus,
Verse/chorus of cumulonimbus clouds passing to the east,

A drum solo of thunder, a lead vocal of heavy, steady rain.

II. Concerning the Identification of Edible Mushrooms

Thurs, Aug 21—This morning's breeze carries woodsmoke
From wildfires near the Army fort where that fundamentalist

Shot up his fellow soldiers. Do you think his figment of Allah
Was pleased, or saddened? Hard to say. My figment of Jesus

Constantly weeps as if he's watching *Terms of Endearment.*
Speaking of movies, I hope to play Allah in an action-packed

Biopic, what with my blond, blue-eyed, devilish good looks.
Imagine all the goddamn smoke that would create! And

My assistant, swallowed up in a Buddha fat-suit, the two of us
Falling from top of the Empire State, each with the other

In a stranglehold. I'm just sayin'. Maybe a sword fight
Atop the Great Wall of China? A speedboat chase

Through south Louisiana swamps? One time in Lafayette,
I flipped the TV back and forth between James Brown's

Dead bloated face and Saddam Hussein's hooded hanging.
Flipped back and forth all night. Hail, high winds outside—

Still flipping. Tornadoes touching down in the Atchafalaya—
Still flipping. Poor Cajuns huddling beneath cypress pirogues—

Still flipping. Like a nightmare I couldn't wake up from. Like
A bad hallucination from Hill Country psilocybin mushrooms.

The most effective ones, as we all know, grow on cow shit.

III. Concerning the Identification of an Eastern Screech Owl

Mon, Oct 11—Why is it when one drives across a bridge
There's this urge to toss out a wallet or a purse

Past the railing? Sometimes eyeglasses. Never
A cellphone, as it's nonessential. Better to pull over,

Get out and jump, methinks. Worked for Berryman.
Having written a book's worth of horrible poems

Called "Creeksongs" before I'd ever read John, am I
Some sort of time-traveling Freshman Lit student,

Unknowing accomplice to his suicide? Huffy
Henry indeed. I do don old-man clothes to spread

My scowl around campus. I do enjoy the odd tipple
At odd hours of the day. And my thickish beard

Is as gray as the baby owl's down. One evening
Last summer, during drought, two juvenile screech owls

Sat atop a telephone pole by our driveway, peeping,
Slow-blinking, shitting mommy-food to the curb.

I seem to recall being pleased with myself, as if
I alone was responsible for this moment. As if

That bourbon on the rocks in my fist was some
Magic elixir, the binoculars around my neck a wizard's

Conjuring tool. All my kingdom laid out before me.

Despite or Because of the Bourbon

This flivver parked inside my chest
Refuses to crank. I fold and unfold
And eat the road map with hot sauce.
Daddy speaks of souse meat. He worries

Up the weather. *This here exit is the exit*
You say as we pass by the exit. Daddy
Speaks of cancer, oak leaves in gutters.
My third eye sparkles like a Kmart

Christmas star. Daddy speaks of car wrecks,
Radiation seeds, sparrows. Black Jesus
Break dances while White Jesus weeps.
I pray myself to sleep and dream hellfire.

Tottenham Street Blues

There's a bell in this toyshop
For my bicycle back home.
I ring it until the owner coughs
And stares me down. Me—

Ugly American, noon-drunk,
Cash-poor in the old empire.
I sway and smile and say, *Sorry*.
Picture postcards sit in a rack,

Stacked bareback, awaiting pub
Scrawls and double-decker jokes.
That Big Ben card I sent days ago
Would not have reached you yet,

Just like this sunlight, so rare here.
I exit empty-handed into cacophony
Of bus roar and moped whine,
Still hearing that little bell chime.

Villanelle for Extinct Birds

The flightless moa, the auk and swamphen
Stare up at me from paintings in a book.
I fluff and squawk when my wife sets in

To point out dirty dishes. *The den's
A mess,* she chirps to my face's dodo look.
Neither flightless moa, auk, nor swamphen

Could ever contemplate my sin
Of sloth, of living for moments. She cooks
Our supper and coos when I begin

Pouring the gin and tonics. *To men
Of earth!* I eagle-shriek, I caw as a rook.
Those flightless auks, moas and swamphens

Were no match for the metal weapons,
The scythes, the tractors, the smokestacks.
We polish off our drinks as I open

Another bottle, another illusion
Of permanence, another toast to bad luck.
The flightless moas, auks and swamphens
Fluffed and squawked and let us win.

English Sonnet for Extinct Birds

As if our words meant more than coos and chirps
My freckled shoulders slump where wings would be.
Like sideshow dodos, we dance to drunken claps
And feather dust funny bones, tickle fancies.
Stop dreaming of Carolina parakeets!
Why can't you leave us well enough alone?
I know if we'd be pecking in the streets
And squawking at cats I'd never be so vain
To think this all must never end. Those flocks
Of pigeons darkened daytime skies. We grabbed
Our guns and so it goes. This nest of sticks
And bricks will topple, and I've wept and held
The tiny broken eggshells in my hand.
That kind of loss I'll never understand.

Ghazal for Extinct Birds

Like the Laysan rail or the Maori bushwren
I forage here flightless in a cold north wind

That strips trees of leaves, that rips words
From chapped lips. Facing downwind

Of traffic, waiting on the bus, I whistle
A trill of springtime fancy. The wind

Abates but I'm late for work. My boss
Is out of town and someone got wind

Of the office party; those donuts won't last
The rest of the day. I catch a second wind

And hunt and peck until lunch. That taco
Stand should not have closed! The wind

Kicks up and shrieks inside the stairwell.
Nothing lasts forever, Whit, not even wind.

Bedtime Story Redux

Listen up, my dear ones. These days
Grow fangs and bark and drool.
They reek of woodsmoke, wet fur.

The past is a rancher's coil spring trap
We all get snared in. Let the howling
Begin! Someone should call the cops

To say it wasn't me. Someone should
Phone the landlord to complain
About the weather. Somewhere

Keeps stretching rubber-band-like
Beyond our driveway. If I could,
I would cosmic dust you far away

To the other side of dreams. There,
We would truth each other. There,
We would feast upon hearts of stars.

Bar Napkin Love Letter

I never know when to stop. Moon
Goes down, sun comes up. North wind
South wind. Alarm clock chimes five.
Ice melting on a blade of grass.
You beside me should mean forever.

You're beside yourself without flowers.
In my dream I'm beside you snoring
In that cold and shabby bedroom
Where we fall asleep clutching books.

If my time left is a high desert to cross
Barefoot like some heartbroken Apache
Your laughter will be a raven's caw.
Your name will be two river pebbles
Held on my tongue to ward off thirst.

Time Out

Send yourself straight to bed
With no TV, with no supper.
Stew in your own savory juices.
Just sit in the corner and stew.
Imagine the sound of angels
Mating. Imagine the sound
Of someone you love saying
I can't keep up this fool's facade.
This is what you end up doing
When the medicine's no good.
This is what you end up getting
For believing in a god only
To deny and defy and curse it.
That cross-eyed little bastard
Who stabbed you in 1st grade?
He's wealthy, happily married
To the prom queen, a couple
Of kids in Ivy League schools.
Just sit and stew. That swarthy
Young fellow on the Paris Metro
Who robbed you, left you shaking?
He sleeps like a baby—never
Felt better. Rolling in filthy lucre
And, at the moment, enjoying
A high-priced Bulgarian call girl.
Cut yourself some slack, though.
Nobody has a clue. There will,
However, be a Q&A following.
There will be time enough for us all.
There will be a light at the end
Of the tunnel, if only someone
Remembers to leave it turned on.

Day After Christmas Blues Poem

And this shall be a sign unto you—
You shall find the leftovers wrapped
In aluminum foil, lying in the refrigerator.
Another gray morning sky, another
Hangover of biblical proportions. Dirty

Dishes, the unlit tree. Two crows rummaging
Through gold and green wrapping paper
The wind blew against the back fence.
Three sheep beyond the back fence,
Standing still in their field, standing

In the manner they've always stood,
In the manner they always will,
Their gentle breath fogging upwards
Only to dissipate. A blessed sun
Beyond gray sky, rising only to fall again.

The Only Apocalypse

> *Time is neither young nor old,*
> *but simply new, always counting...*
> —Wendell Berry

There is a dove on its morning wire
Announcing this very moment,

And I want it to mean something,
Something heavy, as the longhairs used to say.

I want it scrawled in some virgin's blood
All over the cave walls of my mind.

I want it etched into the skulls of our foes.
I want it read in the tea leaves, preserved

Inside every tree ring. I want it bannered on high
From that skywriter's prop plane. I want it

Polluting the groundwater, black as cake
From the old Kentucky coal. I want it

Shouted all at once by the business-suited
Millions on their sidewalks and subways,

In their limos and taxis and Learjets, shouted
As some one-syllable mantra, the quick

Cough from a punch to the solar plexus,
The question to all of our answers.

Notes on the Year's End

Another empty bottle, another circle
Around the sun. Cold floors, catnaps.
Stew meat simmers in the red wine.

Leaves drift against a chain-link fence,
Gray sky backdrops bare-branch fingers.
What disappears reappears—rain,

High school friends, crumpled twenties
In the pea coat's pocket. That bald
Eagle east of Little Rock, dozing

In a riverbend cypress. Midnight passing
The delta. Wet snowflakes on his head
Feathers—white upon white upon white...

Acknowledgments

Some of these poems have been published in their current state, or an earlier one, in the following journals, to whose editors grateful acknowledgment is given:

Arcadia Magazine
Bone Parade
Carolina Quarterly
Cold Mountain Review
Concho River Review
Cumberland River Review
december
Foxing Quarterly
Mississippi Review
Monarch Review
Off The Coast
Penny Ante Feud
The Stillwater Review

Thanks to all family, friends, and loved ones, but especially to Aunt June, who told me to be sure and spell "god" with a capital G.

Cover photo by Harold Whit Williams
Author photo by Ashley Savage Williams
Cover and interior book design by Diane Kistner
Baskerville text and Benguiat Gothic titling

About FutureCycle Press

FutureCycle Press is dedicated to publishing lasting English-language poetry books, chapbooks, and anthologies in both print-on-demand and ebook formats. Founded in 2007 by long-time independent editor/publishers and partners Diane Kistner and Robert S. King, the press incorporated as a nonprofit in 2012. A number of our editors are distinguished poets and writers in their own right, and we have been actively involved in the small press movement going back to the early seventies.

The FutureCycle Poetry Book Prize and honorarium is awarded annually for the best full-length volume of poetry we publish in a calendar year. Introduced in 2013, our Good Works projects are anthologies devoted to issues of universal significance, with all proceeds donated to a related worthy cause. Our Selected Poems series highlights contemporary poets with a substantial body of work to their credit; with this series we strive to resurrect work that has had limited distribution and is now out of print.

We are dedicated to giving all of the authors we publish the care their work deserves, making our catalog of titles the most diverse and distinguished it can be, and paying forward any earnings to fund more great books.

We've learned a few things about independent publishing over the years. We've also evolved a unique, resilient publishing model that allows us to focus mainly on vetting and preserving for posterity the most books of exceptional quality without becoming overwhelmed with bookkeeping and mailing, fundraising activities, or taxing editorial and production "bubbles." To find out more about what we are doing, come see us at www.futurecycle.org.

The FutureCycle Poetry Book Prize

All full-length volumes of poetry published by FutureCycle Press in a given calendar year are considered for the annual FutureCycle Poetry Book Prize. This allows us to consider each submission on its own merits, outside of the context of a contest. Too, the judges see the finished book, which will have benefitted from the beautiful book design and strong editorial gloss we are famous for.

The book ranked the best in judging is announced as the prize-winner in the subsequent year. There is no fixed monetary award; instead, the winning poet receives an honorarium of 20% of the total net royalties from all poetry books and chapbooks the press sold online in the year the winning book was published. The winner is also accorded the honor of being on the panel of judges for the next year's competition; all judges receive copies of all contending books to keep for their personal library.